ODE TO JOY

ODE TO JOY

CRAIG LUCAS

THEATRE COMMUNICATIONS GROUP   NEW YORK   2016

Ode to Joy is published by Theatre Communications Group, Inc., 520 Eighth Avenue, 24th Floor, New York, NY 10018-4156

The publication of *Ode to Joy* by Craig Lucas, through TCG's Book Program, is made possible in part by the New York State Council on the Arts with the support of Governor Andrew Cuomo and the New York State Legislature.

TCG books are exclusively distributed to the book trade by Consortium Book Sales and Distribution.

LIBRARY OF CONGRESS CATALOGING-IN-PUBLICATION DATA

Lucas, Craig, author.
Ode to joy / Craig Lucas.
First edition.
ISBN 9781559364928 (softcover)
ISBN 9781559368063 (ebook)
DDC 812/.54—dc23

Book design and composition by Lisa Govan
Cover design by Mark Melnick
Cover artwork: Craig Hawkins, *Supervention No.15*, 2014.
Acrylic with monotype on paper, 11 x 14 in. (Artwork partly composed of a reproduction of Robert Longo's *Untitled*, 1981.)

First Edition, September 2016

Ode to Joy is for Nico Muhly

———————

ACKNOWLEDGMENTS

O*de to Joy* was commissioned by the Greenfield Prize at the Hermitage Artist Retreat in Englewood, Florida.

The Hermitage Artist Retreat invites artists and writers in every discipline to work at its historic site on Florida's Gulf of Mexico. The Hermitage commissions the Greenfield Prize to bring into the world works of art that will have a significant impact on the broad as well as the artistic culture of our society.

The play was completed under a commission from Playwrights Horizons.

I would like to acknowledge the generous time and energies of Bruce Rodgers, Patricia Caswell, Sharyn Lonsdale, Greg Leaming, Michael Edwards, Jason Bradley, Hannah Goalstone, Elizabeth Marvel, Bill Camp, Tim Sanford and Christian Parker. Thanks to dramaturg Sydne Mahone, who knows how to ask the right questions at the right time. And a deep bow of gratitude to the man who believed in the play before it was whole—may there always be artistic directors of such quality—David Van Asselt.

ODE TO JOY

PRODUCTION HISTORY

Ode to Joy was presented by Rattlestick Playwrights Theater (David Van Asselt, Artistic Director; Brian Long, Managing Director) at the Cherry Lane Theatre in New York City, on February 27, 2014. It was directed by the author. The scenic design was by Andrew Boyce, the costume design was by Catherine Zuber, the lighting design was by Paul Whitaker, the sound design was by Daniel Kluger; the production stage manager was Michael Denis. The cast was:

ADELE	Kathryn Erbe
BILL	Arliss Howard
MALA	Roxanna Hope

CHARACTERS

ADELE, a painter; determined, playful, intimidatingly bright, alert, deeply kind, sometimes combative; an alcoholic; anywhere from late thirties to mid-fifties

BILL, a cardiac surgeon; born into wealth, classically educated, erudite, hardworking, passionate, somewhat solitary, widely traveled and experienced in a variety of milieus; an alcoholic; anywhere from late thirties to mid-fifties

MALA, a pharmaceutical executive; fiercely ambitious, private, wounded somehow, refuses to speak of past trauma; a nondrinker; anywhere from thirty to fifty

The actor playing Mala also plays Bartender. The actor playing Bill also plays TV Voice and Dr. Wong.

NOTES

Pauses can be brief.

Words in brackets are not spoken.

Slashes indicate possible points of overlap for the subsequent speaker.

An ungrammatical comma is a hitch in the thinking or rhythm.

SCENE 1

Adele's building. Day, 2014.

Adele is alone. She holds a paintbrush and is working on a large canvas (unseen) between herself and the audience. Soon she is overcome with physical pain.

ADELE: This is the story of how the pain goes away. Or: how I got out of the way . . . of me and everyone else . . . Once upon a time, seven years ago, a Thursday afternoon . . .

(She closes her eyes and a bar begins to glow with warmth. She walks into it.)

SCENE 2

Bar. Night, 2007.

Bill is seated at the bar. Adele approaches the bar, receives a text, types, tries to get the bartender's attention. The bar is not officially open and the bartender has headphones on.

ADELE: May I . . . ?

(Adele types. A very sad song is playing. Bill sobs. Beat.)

(To the bartender) Yes, could I have a double vodka on the rocks and could you put on something . . . a little—less—something *joyful*, thank you. *(To Bill)* Would—? I'm Adele. Would you like to talk about it? . . . I understand. Would you like me to leave you be? *(Receives text)* Oh, please. *(Types)* I'll just tell you what I would tell myself. Whatever it is— Things have a way of changing. They look impossibly scary at the time and then . . . at some point . . . through the whatever you may be . . . I'm not saying life isn't tragic . . . You also realize there are wonderful things that would never, could never have happened if the first thing . . . Right?

BILL: I'm Bill.

ADELE: Hi, Bill. Would it . . . help to tell me what happened? *(Receives text)* Oh my God. *(Typing)* Some people make the simplest thing into a, paragraph of tax code. Sometimes it helps to just say it; it doesn't seem so terrible.

BILL: My wife committed suicide; she was six months pregnant with our first child. We tried and tried.

ADELE: Oh God. / That's—

BILL: But that doesn't vitiate your point.

(Short pause.)

That song, that's all.

ADELE: Oh my—

BILL: And I think . . . Well, I may have cancer. Yeah.

ADELE: What kind?

BILL: Prostate.

ADELE: Oh, isn't that the kind now, don't they have very good
    results if they catch it early?

BILL: Yes.

ADELE: Did they . . . ?

BILL: No.

ADELE: Oh.

BILL: I mean they haven't even gotten to the point of saying it
    is cancer, it / might be.

ADELE: I see, good.

BILL: It isn't, I'm sure it isn't.

ADELE: Oh good. No. But just the . . . Did he forget my drink?

BILL: I think that's it. I think he's she.

ADELE: I think you're right. On both counts. *(To the bartender)*
    Could I—? . . .

BARTENDER: Could you wait a sec? / We aren't actually open
    just yet.

ADELE: Yeah, I / *waited*, I think you al—

BILL: She waited already! You poured it.

ADELE: She doesn't care. I'm glad to meet you.

BILL: I'll know in a few days, it's just the cumulative . . . the . . .
    seeing you . . .

ADELE: Me?

BILL: . . . so obviously in love.

ADELE: Oh, I'm not in love.

BILL: Well, in something . . . with . . .

ADELE: No, no, I'm in— *(Receives text)* Habit. That's what I—

(The music disappears.)

Oh, thank God. They say you can't love a depressed person, because they're too in love with their crappy narrative.

BILL: Uh-huh.

ADELE: Don't worry, she will bring it. The same way you can't really have a relationship with a corporate lawyer. They're too busy fucking everybody else to give it to you with any—

BILL: Uh-huh.

ADELE: —real verve. I'm lucky enough to have both. What do you do? Sorry.

BILL: I'm a / doctor.

(Beethoven's "Ode to Joy" plays loudly, overlapping and obliterating the word "doctor.")

ADELE: Ow.

(The music stops, then is replaced again by bar music.)

That was . . . *(To the bartender)* Very funny! She'll get it, don't . . .

(Bill offers a sip of his drink.)

Thank you. Mm, what is that?

BILL: Scotch.

ADELE: I never drink scotch.

BILL: Well now you have a new vice.

ADELE: You don't have prostate cancer, Bill.

BILL: How can you tell?

ADELE: I can just tell. You are a winner. You don't. I— Well, I don't want to— Let's just say I have powers.

BILL: You do? What kind of powers do you have?

ADELE: Oh, all kinds. She'll bring it, she's not going to forget.

BILL: She *has* forgotten.

ADELE: No, my powers tell me that any second she is going to remember that drink and bring it.

BILL: . . . I'm gonna get you your fucking drink.

(Bill climbs over the bar.)

ADELE: No no no. / Bill. *Bill.*

BARTENDER: You're not allowed behind / the bar.

BILL: I *am* allowed here because you left her drink to languish in sorrow and she is thirsty— It's okay, forgiveness is / the key to everything.

ADELE: Thank you! Thanks!

BILL: I have powers, too.

ADELE: Yes you do.

BILL *(Toasts)*: To winners.

ADELE *(Toasts)*: Winners.

BILL: Consistent winners. To those who hit the bull's-eye every time. It is inconsistency that drives us truly mad—

ADELE: Yes.

BILL: If you reward a rat for performing a certain task, its brain shows an increased level of dopamine.

ADELE: I love dopamine.

BILL: The next time it's required to perform the task, the dopamine goes up in anticipation of the reward.

ADELE: Oh. That makes sense.

BILL: But if you don't—say thirty percent of the time—then when it's asked to perform the task, it rewards *itself* even more.

ADELE: It does?

BILL: It's the uncertainty it's palliating.

ADELE: Ohhh.

BILL: Yeah.

ADELE: Wow.

BILL: Gambling. Any addiction. Superstition, religion . . . all tied to the same bullshit.

ADELE: How—? Explain that, I get the gambling.

BILL: Take a couple of rats—

ADELE: Oh, I dated 'em. Go on.

BILL: —put 'em in separate cages, reward them at arbitrary moments. Whatever each is doing before being rewarded, the rat assumes that's the thing that caused the reward; it will go on doing it from then on out. Father, Son, and Holy Ghost.

ADELE: You don't believe in God.

BILL: No. You?

ADELE: No, I . . . Yeeeah, I don't know, yeah, I think, I— Yeah, I do.

BILL: Are you sure?

ADELE: No. But I think we're supposed to wrestle with it. No?

BILL: Kierkegaard.

ADELE: Is that who it is?

BILL: Did you know people who believe in God are less apt to be depressed or commit suicide.

ADELE: They are?

BILL: What do you do?

ADELE: I'm interested. I'm a painter, but— No, I am.

BILL: I believe you.

ADELE: Interested, go on.

BILL: You have a gallery?

ADELE: No. I have a minuscule coterie of insane fans who love my work but who might just be saying that to keep me from hurling myself off a building; I barely eke by; but I've never heard—

BILL: Where's your studio?

ADELE: I'm oh I'm in transition right now. I'm moving.

BILL: In or out?

ADELE: Well, it's always both, isn't it?

BILL: Very good. How can I see them?

ADELE: But I do want to get back to Kierkegaard.

BILL: No one wants that.

ADELE *(Glances at her cell phone)*: Sixteen messages. In, what? How could I dare not be waiting on each minute fluctuation in his internal . . .

BILL: Inconsistency.

ADELE: Oh yeah.

BILL: Love's a gamble. Right, not love. Habit. They say in AA—

(Adele finds photos on her cell phone and shows them to Bill.)

This yours? . . . They're . . . These are very . . . I've never seen anything like them. How do you do that? The reflection where . . .

ADELE: Oh, yeah, that's— . . . I . . . Complicated.

BILL: How big?

ADELE: Too big. Eight-by-ten . . . Hard to sell.

BILL: There's no boundary between—

ADELE: Yeah. A lot of painting is about outlines and boundaries, but . . .

BILL: I'd love to see in person.

ADELE: Well.

BILL: I'd like to buy one.

ADELE: Oh. Well.

BILL: I would.

ADELE: What do they say in AA?

BILL: I would, Adele.

ADELE: . . . Well. You're—

BILL: I'm not drunk.

ADELE: No, I mean they take up a lot of space.

BILL: That might be your problem, right there.

ADELE: What?

BILL: Somebody says I'd like to buy one, you say, "Well . . . "

ADELE: Well . . . You just meet someone, you don't—

BILL: I may have a lot of space. I may have more than one home, and considerable wall space in various parts of the globe . . . Which . . . I . . .

ADELE: That must be nice.

BILL: It's all I've known.

ADELE: That must be nice too. Or not.

BILL: A man with a lot of blank wall space crying out for paintings to hang in plain view of other potential art patrons is not something / to sneer at.

ADELE: Did I sneeze? *(Correcting herself)* Sneed— *(Correcting)* I s'*nei*[ther]— *(Tries again, with much deliberateness)* I *neither* sneered nor sneezed.

BILL: You said sneed and snide.

ADELE: Yes. I did. Do you want to make something of that, Bill? This drink is not going to be nearly enough.

BILL: I don't think so.

ADELE: Oh, forget it, she won't be back for another week.

BILL: I know you didn't ask for a diagnosis. But . . .

ADELE: Well. Depends on what you charge.

BILL: I'm expensive.

ADELE: Oh. Well, me, too.

BILL: Good.

ADELE: Bub. What do they say in AA?

BILL: You're fun. Adele.

ADELE: And then Kierkegaard, you're fun, too.

BILL: Have you read Kierkegaard?

ADELE: No, that's why I'm depending on you, have you?

BILL: Yes.

ADELE: Why?

BILL: Exactly.

ADELE: No, why?

BILL: Because Kierkegaard wrote interestingly on some subjects I'm interested—

ADELE: Like?

BILL: Like irony. Most especially.

ADELE: What *is* irony?

BILL: Oh come on.

ADELE: Wait, I'll look it up.

BILL: No no, don't do that.

ADELE: I have the OED, for just this—

BILL: No, it's wrong, it has the wrong definition.

ADELE: What do you mean?

BILL: People use the word incorrectly.

ADELE: Well, if it's in the dictionary—

BILL: That means that's how people use it but it isn't what I nor Kierkegaard mean when we speak of irony, as we do often quietly in the dark.

ADELE: No?

BILL: No.

ADELE: It's a secret definition.

BILL: Kierkegaard suggests that irony is a slight—it's a discrepancy between the expected and a . . .

ADELE: The juxtaposition.

BILL: . . . an invitation to stop

ADELE: Uh-huh.

BILL: . . . and question.

ADELE: Oh. Cool.

BILL: And that the greatest, most refined or elegant or profound expression of irony means exactly what is said on an important level . . . So when Socrates says, "Death may be the greatest of all human blessings," or Kierkegaard asks, "Is there a single Christian in all of Christendom?" he doesn't just mean—

ADELE: Goes to church and blames Jews.

BILL: Exactly.

ADELE: And why are Christians so pissed about, I mean, even if Jews had killed Christ, it was only for like two days!

BILL: Irony. That. It's a kind of a seeking, it's not snarkiness. But— . . .

ADELE: And you remember this, how long ago did you read Kierkegaard?

BILL: I have returned to him.

ADELE: Lately?

BILL: Yes.

ADELE: And you're an atheist?

BILL: Yes.

ADELE: . . . What do they say in AA? Do you go?

BILL: They, AA, say the definition of insanity is doing the same thing over and over expecting different results, but really, people drink because they know the result.

ADELE: Consistency.

BILL: Exactly. My wife was an alcoholic.

ADELE: I like that you cried . . . That's attractive to me. You didn't hide your face. You didn't run out . . . Are you in anything now?

BILL: In?

ADELE: Is that rude to ask? . . .

BILL: I don't know what . . .

ADELE: Any movies or plays? You look familiar. From TV?

BILL: I'm a cardiac surgeon.

ADELE: I thought you—you said doctor, I thought you said actor.

BILL: We discussed my fees, Adele.

ADELE: I know, but I thought we were theoretically granting you a psychiatric license, which actually was a veiled reference—

BILL: To?

ADELE: Well, there was a double entendre thing going on too, wasn't—? Yes, there was! I thought you said actor.

BILL: You're fun and you're beautiful.

ADELE: You're drunk.

BILL: No.

ADELE: Well . . . Do people want to talk about love when they come to see you about their heart?

BILL: Yes.

ADELE: Of course.

BILL: How did you know that?

ADELE: Doctors aren't trained to deal with people dying or certainly not with getting sick themselves.

BILL: I don't have cancer. How do you know all this?

ADELE: I knew someone who had a heart transplant . . .

BILL: Who?

ADELE *(Indeterminate gesture)*: When'd she die?

BILL: Who was the doctor?

(Adele shrugs.)

Six years ago. Tomorrow.

ADELE: Oh . . . I hate anniversaries. I do not get it.

BILL: Consistency.

ADELE: You want to know why I hate New Year's?

BILL: Why? That's her portrait, by the way.

ADELE: That's your wife?

BILL: She and her brother owned this place. I live upstairs.

ADELE: She's very pretty.

BILL: Thank you.

ADELE: Remember Y2K?

BILL: Of course.

ADELE: She is, beautiful.

BILL: Thank you.

ADELE: My significant other at the time and I were sure it was going to be like Armageddon—

BILL: Uh-huh.

ADELE: We were so prepared—we bought a generator, we had so many canned tamales. Okay, midnight . . . nothing.

BILL: Right.

ADELE: She turns to me as if the words had arrived in the mail two days ago and she just remembered to hand them to me: "I want to break up." Now that I was no longer needed to provide solace and warmth and—

BILL: Nice.

ADELE: —to get her through the dissolution of civilization, and I'm leaving out— Anyway, you know, I am somehow responsible for her doomsday disappointment . . . So.

(Bill stares at the photo behind the bar.)

BILL: One mythic bitch.

ADELE: No.

BILL: Mmmm. One true Cunt-tress of Cuntitude.

ADELE: No no—

BILL: A shameless, soul-killing—

ADELE: She was actually a very good person.

BILL: You knew my wife?

ADELE: Oh—sorry, I'm— Oh, she was? Oh. That's too bad.

BILL: That's what's hard when they die.

ADELE: Yes.

BILL: Like that.

ADELE: Yes.

BILL: They die *at* you.

ADELE: Yes.

BILL: OCD.

ADELE: Oh.

BILL: Total and . . . Everything had to be, this way, that, no meds quite ever got to the—

ADELE: Oh.

BILL: And it's horrible, it's no way to live—

ADELE: God.

BILL: These people are paralyzed with rituals and doubt. I couldn't save her, and I couldn't bring myself to leave her, and she knew it, and I was going to pay.

ADELE: That's . . . very / hard.

(Adele's cell phone rings. She doesn't answer.)

BILL: You don't want to— / . . . just . . . ?

ADELE: One of the wonderful things about meeting you, Bill?

BILL: Yessss? You want another?

ADELE: Sure.

BILL *(To the bartender)*: Another round?

ADELE: Is that I actually have something more interesting to occupy me than whatever new fecal drippings are being flung my way via— Sorry, that was a little . . .

BILL: Vivid.

ADELE: Yeah, but: consistency.

BILL: Maybe you should stick to women.

ADELE: No. I stick to men. There was only one woman. Mala.

BILL: That should have been the clue right / there.

ADELE: I know.

BILL: It means nasty.

ADELE: I like 'em nasty. Why don't you have someone?

BILL: I date.

ADELE: Oh, good.

BILL: Every single one turns out to be insane. And they don't seem it. At first.

ADELE: Not good.

BILL: No. I think, you know: This could work. This might be love. Is this love?

ADELE: Uh-huh.

BILL: But how do you know if it is? How do you really know? . . . No, I'm—

ADELE: Oh, you're asking? You know how?

BILL: How?

ADELE: When other people say to you, "Honey, you realize he's missing several important teeth," and: You don't care!

BILL: Uh-huh.

ADELE: I think you have to be delusional, that's when you know, because everybody's missing something. And it's . . . the sense that you have to get into, toward, through to . . . past . . .

BILL: Yes.

ADELE: You have to get it. You have to get at it!

BILL: I'm feeling it.

ADELE: You are?

BILL: Plato said basically it's impossible to know, when you're in love, if the love emanates from the other person or something in yourself.

(Adele starts typing on her cell phone.)

What are you doing?

ADELE: Looking up "love."

BILL: Don't do that.

ADELE: Why?

BILL: Because it won't be right. Stop. Put it away. You know what love is. It isn't a word. It isn't in there.

ADELE: Okay.

BILL: You know what it is.

ADELE: . . . I want to get a dog.

BILL: Me, too.

ADELE: What are you going to name your dog?

BILL: Marcus Aurelius.

ADELE: That's a great name.

BILL: I think children are overrated.

ADELE: I do, too.

BILL: I never wanted them.

ADELE: Me either. What kind of dog?

BILL: Wirehaired dachshund.

(Adele wants the same breed; Bill reacts:)

Shut up.

ADELE: They're much calmer and friendlier with other dogs—

BILL: They are.

ADELE: —than the smooth haired. Did you know that they're the only certified breed that hunts—

BILL: Yes.

ADELE: —above and below ground.

BILL: I did. / In fact—

ADELE: They live a long time, though.

BILL: They do.

ADELE: Like easily sixteen years.

BILL: Yes they do.

ADELE: So you have to want to live.

BILL: Who said I didn't want to live?

ADELE: I'm just saying—they're a commitment.

BILL: I went to medical school. I stayed married to an insane person.

ADELE: Okay.

BILL: I was a classics major, I read Greek, I had a degree in philosophy before I set foot in medicine, I think I've proved—

ADELE: Yes, okay.

BILL: —I'm not afraid of commitment . . . You mean to survive if— You said I didn't have cancer—

ADELE: You don't.

BILL: You said you have powers.

ADELE: I do. Can I do a search? Can I see if there's a breeder with—? I don't want to make too many assumptions . . . You didn't have to even bother with school, did you?

BILL: In my family you did. In my family you made a contribution.

ADELE: Do you know how rare that is? This is the best moment. My favorite. Okay, I found us a breeder. They have a litter! And one male left, I'm calling. Okay? *(She dials the cell phone)*

BILL: Yeah, yeah. What did you mean? The best moment. Yes.

ADELE: It was a slip.

BILL: What did it reveal?

ADELE: It meant . . . At the top of the hill. When you can see the coast all the way down, know how easy it's going to be . . . It's the greatest . . . the hovering before liftoff, before the long effortless slide . . . Setting forth. Do you know what I'm talking about? Really? Is that cool I—? *(Into cell phone)* Hi! My name is Adele? Do you still have the male dachshund pup? You do? I'll take him. Yeah. No, I'll take him. I want him. Do you have a pen? Okay, I'll give you my MasterCard—

BILL *(To the bartender)*: Could we—? Yeah, why don't you make it two for each of us, that way we won't have to bother you . . . Great.

ADELE: We'll pick him up tomorrow. Thank you so much. *(She hangs up)* Done. What else?

BILL: Do you like the country?

ADELE: Yes, why?

BILL: I have a place in Fairfield County.

ADELE: You do? That's not the country.

BILL: No? Do you like to garden?

ADELE: I've never had a chance.

BILL: Are you feeling it? Is it just the booze?

ADELE: Who cares? If we're both drinking.

BILL: That's irony.

ADELE: It is?

BILL: The most ironic thing of all is no one knows the true definition.

ADELE: It's much easier to housebreak a dog in the country. But can you take the time off?

BILL: I'll come on weekends. You can paint.

ADELE: No. I don't want to be away from you.

BILL: It's good, distance is good.

ADELE: Oh, it's too soon.

BILL: Play it by ear.

ADELE: I want to play it by ear.

BILL: Can I call your father and ask for his blessing?

ADELE *(Hands Bill the cell phone)*: Your funeral. Oh, this'll kill it. / No—

(She tries to get the cell phone back.)

BILL: Hi, Misss / ter—

ADELE: McLermy.

BILL: McLermy? No, no, this is Dr. William Rubenstein. No, sir, I'm calling to ask if I might have your daughter's hand in marriage. In ma— He hung up on me.

ADELE: Now you know all there is to know about my family. What Kierkegaard do I start with?

BILL: I'll show you.

ADELE: I think grief takes its own sweet time, Bill.

BILL: Yes it does.

ADELE: I don't think you were ready.

BILL: I don't think I was.

ADELE: But maybe you are now.

BILL: Maybe.

ADELE: We own a puppy.

BILL: We own a puppy.

BILL AND ADELE: Marcus.

ADELE *(Puppy voice)*: Little Marcus.

BILL: No voices.

ADELE: Yes! You can't have a puppy without voices. May . . . may I—?

BILL: Yes, you may.

(They kiss.)

(Puppy voice) All right.

ADELE: . . . You're just goofing around on me.

BILL: Are you?

ADELE: No.

BILL: Are you sure?

ADELE: Are you?

BILL: It's happened enough times, I should recognize it.

ADELE: Me, too. You slipped right past all the gates and flares—

BILL: You, too.

ADELE: —and "no-fuckin'-ways"—

BILL: You, too.

ADELE: The whole computer system, in, out. My whole—

BILL: You, too.

ADELE: —body.

BILL: A direct hit! Three cherries!

ADELE: Really?

BILL: All systems go!

ADELE: Really? . . . Where will it end?

BILL: *What?!* No, shhh! / Nooooo!

ADELE: What? What what . . . ?

BILL: Are you insane? We haven't—

ADELE: What?

BILL: "Where will it end?" You know where. / Don't—

ADELE: Where?

BILL: Where everything ends. Stop.

ADELE: Oh.

BILL: Three things that will not survive irony—

ADELE: Okay.

BILL: Suffering. Religious ecstasy. *Passion.*

ADELE: Okay . . . But—

BILL: HALT! Go back! / No no.

ADELE: —you said, "You / *know* where."

BILL: Abandon hope all ye who enter there!

ADELE: Wh—?

BILL: Adele?

ADELE: The bartender's—

BILL: Fuck 'er, Adele, may I kiss you?

ADELE: It . . . depends.

BILL: No it doesn't.

ADELE: It does.

BILL: Why does it depend? What does it depend on?

ADELE: Depends where.

BILL: . . . Where indeed . . . *Where will it end?*

ADELE: Where?

(A knock.)

BILL: What? . . . Hey.

ADELE *(To us)*: So that's Bill.

BILL: The past come knocking?

ADELE: My former studio? Eight years before meeting Bill.

(Bill remains seated at the bar throughout:)

SCENE 3

Adele's former studio. Day, 1999.
    Adele opens the door to reveal Mala.

MALA: I'm so sorry I'm late.

ADELE: It's okay.

MALA: And I can't stay very long, oh God, I'm already late for my next . . .

ADELE: Would you like to make it another time?

MALA: No no no, God no.

ADELE: Okay, if you're . . .

MALA: Oh, this is pretty, this one, oh wow.

ADELE: Yeah, that's uh . . . Just a primed canvas . . . That isn't . . .

MALA: Oh. Well. "Sold!"

ADELE: That's a wash of pigment.

MALA: It's very pretty.

ADELE: These are all new.

MALA: Okay. I'm ready.

(Silence.)

This? . . . Is so . . .

ADELE: Yeah.

MALA: . . . disturbing.

ADELE: Oh.

MALA: Euww.

(Silence.)

ADELE: Well . . . I don't know what Judy told you about the work but . . .

MALA: Did someone like lock you in a trunk of a car on acid when you were five or something?

ADELE: Nnnnnot exactly.

MALA: That's . . . Who are all those people, are those supposed to be . . .

(Short pause.)

Are . . . ?

(Silence.)

ADELE: To be . . . ?

MALA: I'm sorry, that is . . . I want something to hang in my home. Where I live. This isn't for a slaughterhouse. This isn't for frightening refugees from crossing the border.

ADELE: I . . .

MALA: I do not understand why people make art that upsets other people. I am sorry.

ADELE: I . . . don't think you should apologize. It's very personal.

MALA: Well, I feel attacked. I feel assaulted.

ADELE: I don't think you should buy it then.

MALA: Do you have anything . . .

ADELE: . . . This is . . .

(Silence.)

They're very big.

MALA: Big isn't a problem . . . I have space. But . . . Well, are there more? . . . My *God.* I mean . . . Do you have something . . . without . . . uh, dread?

ADELE: With— . . . ?

MALA: Do you have anything . . . serene? Or . . .

ADELE: Serene?

MALA: Joyful?

ADELE: Um . . . I don't really . . . ?

MALA: Something inviting? Something life-uh-embracing?

ADELE: I think this is very . . .

MALA: Something that . . . Would make me want to suppress the suicidal impulse? . . . What's over here?

ADELE: These are studies?

MALA: Let me see . . . What's this? . . . Holy Christ.

ADELE: Not to your . . . ?

MALA: What is that?

ADELE: That's . . . Well, what does it . . . What do you think it is?

MALA: I think it's some sort of a *fistula*, some kind of . . . aberrant, botched surgical—it's a torture victim. I think it's hostile. I think you . . . bring people up here to frighten them.

ADELE: I don't . . . do that.

MALA: How much is this?

ADELE: I don't sell the studies.

MALA: How much are these?

ADELE: That is five thousand.

MALA: Dollars? Do you have . . . Look, do you have anything . . . ?

ADELE: In taupe? Oh, are you looking for something more in a saffron?

MALA: Are you mocking me?

ADELE: No, you want something to make you feel good about yourself.

MALA: Yes.

ADELE: There's nothing wrong with that.

MALA: I don't think there is.

ADELE: No. But you don't want a painting. You want an enema.

MALA: Okay.

ADELE: You want a fluffer.

MALA: Nice.

ADELE: A pharmaceutical lift. You want a complimentary shiatsu.

MALA: Wait—

ADELE: A round-trip—

MALA: Wait—

ADELE: —all-expenses-paid—

MALA: Wait one minute now.

ADELE: I waited forty-five . . .

MALA: I am the customer.

ADELE: And you are what's wrong with the . . .

MALA: Oh, I am. With what?

ADELE: You. Are what's *in* the painting. Each and every one. That is you staring out, staring back at you.

MALA: I could buy a mirror, then.

ADELE: No, that will lie, that's why it's so so much cheaper. You pay me to tell you the truth. The way you pay a whore to leave when you're done. That's what you're getting. That's the bargain. You see what's real, what's actually *there*, the good and the bad, and if that's not what you want, then stop right next door and pick up a bottle of peppered vodka and knock yourself out.

(Mala leaves. Then the door to the studio reopens.)

MALA *(Reenters)*: Can I ask you one question?

ADELE: By all means.

MALA: How many of these have you sold? . . . None.

ADELE: That would / be—

MALA: None.

ADELE: . . . none / of—

MALA: *YES!!!*

ADELE: —your business.

MALA: None.

ADELE: Of your business.

MALA: You talk about the truth.

ADELE: I've sold paintings.

MALA: Uh-huh.

ADELE: Judy has one, but what I will not sell . . .

MALA: Please. Enlighten me.

ADELE: . . . is myself short.

MALA: Contorted grammar aside, what are you doing later?

ADELE: And, why?

MALA: Are you free this evening?

ADELE: I . . . *am* free this / evening—

MALA: Would you like to have dinner with me?

ADELE: I would put it on the list—

MALA: Done.

ADELE: —right after removing my own teeth with shit-covered pliers and blowing all of my father's golf buddies.

MALA: Well, you have beautiful teeth, so don't do that, and I am much much more satisfying than anyone's golf buddies.

ADELE: I think I should be the judge of that.

MALA: Seven?

ADELE: Don't be late.

MALA: I like you.

(*Mala leaves.*)

ADELE: Trouble . . . Trouble trouble trouble.

(*The door reopens.*)

MALA (*Reenters*): I heard that.

(*They kiss.*)

Hang on. (*Hits speed dial*) Call Silverman and tell him I've had an absolute emergency, order without me, I'll be there in twenty. It's none of your business. (*Hangs up*) Can we turn those paintings around so at least they're not staring at us?

ADELE: No. And twenty is an insult to my allure.

MALA: Yes. Well, I should probably be the judge of that.

(*They kiss.*)

Someone's been celebrating.

(They start to make out.)

You paint drunk?

ADELE: Francis Bacon sips champagne all day long while he paints.

MALA: Whoever that is, I'm sure he can afford to do what he wants.

ADELE: Oh, so money is the determining factor.

MALA: Shut up.

BILL: Hey.

BILL AND MALA: Where'd you go?

ADELE *(To us)*: An expensive restaurant—that same night.

SCENE 4

A restaurant. Later that same night, 1999.
   Mala and Adele sit.

MALA: I can still like you.

ADELE: They're me, they come from me—

MALA: This is what is called Gay Panic.

ADELE: —just as your not liking them is you. You don't really like me.

MALA: How many girlfriends have you had?

ADELE: None.

MALA: Of my business?

ADELE: Are you hot?

MALA: Mmmm.

ADELE: No, seriously.

MALA: I was inoculated for hepatitis, typhoid, meningitis.

ADELE: What did Judy tell you about me?

MALA: I'm going to Turkey.

ADELE: Oh. / Listen—

MALA: Tomorrow.

ADELE: Uh-huh.

MALA: See? You're disappointed, want to come?

ADELE: No, I can't.

MALA: There will plenty of opportunities, I work for a drug company. I used to be a nurse, but I started having problems with my skin—allergies to latex, I couldn't wear the gloves—the best thing that ever happened to me, from bedpans to first class—

ADELE: Good, but—

MALA: —but this, I'm extra-sensitive to most—I don't take drugs.

ADELE: Good. You have a . . . bit of a rash . . .

MALA: Oh, congratulations!

ADELE: What?

MALA: I assume you saw . . . Didn't your friends call you?

ADELE: What?

MALA: You didn't see the paper?

ADELE: No, what?

MALA: I have it.

(Mala produces a newspaper.)

ADELE: Did he . . . ? Oh, he fucking hates me.

MALA: Not by my lights.

ADELE: I don't think I should read it.

MALA: It's very flattering. He says—

ADELE *(Covering her ears)*: No no no.

MALA: —"Supremely talented"?

ADELE: He's been saying that for years.

MALA: You don't want to . . . ?

ADELE: What else does he say?

MALA: "Technical mastery . . . major—" blah blah . . .

ADELE: No, what's the blah blah?

MALA: Well, he had some is / sues—

ADELE: Forget it.

MALA: Those are beautiful quotes.

ADELE: Put it away.

MALA: He has to slather you with praise / exclusively?

ADELE: Yes! If I want to sell anything or be collected or in a museum, even Newark, even Portland, those people don't / buy anything . . .

MALA: The paintings *are* confusing.

ADELE: I feel sick, I don't think this is—

MALA: And given your ability to capture light and all sorts of things he acknowledges, they're also . . .

ADELE: What? What are they?

MALA: I don't remember the exact / word . . .

(Adele snatches the newspaper.)

ADELE: It took me six years to get into this show, I could hang all of three works.

(The waiter starts to approach.)

MALA: A little more time.

(The waiter retreats.)

Paint smaller!

ADELE *(Scans review, wild-eyed)*: You understand I will not ever be able to erase any of what is written here because—

MALA: Oh, / don't be that way—

ADELE: —it is going to become received wisdom unless . . . Oh, great. "Overall, a disappointing—"

MALA: You're concentrating on the negative.

ADELE: Do you understand what that means? . . .

MALA: It means you have work to do.

ADELE: "Familiar tortured flesh with inflammation and rashes" . . . That's what reminded you!

(Adele stands and starts to look for the coat check.)

MALA: Sit down!

ADELE: It does not mean I have more work / to do, it means—

MALA: Lower your voice.

ADELE: —I sell nothing!

MALA: I'll buy one! So—

ADELE: I will make nothing in the next year or two or four or ever—

MALA: I'll make my friends buy them.

ADELE: And my paintings are big, they can't be—

MALA: Make them smaller.

ADELE: I don't decide what size they're going to be.

MALA: You have a court order or / something?

ADELE: I don't even decide on the content.

MALA: So you have a gallery then.

ADELE: No, I—you wouldn't under— *(Looking for the waiter)* Never mind . . . / Could I . . . ?

MALA: I wouldn't understand? *(Her words slowing)* Were you really—?

(Before she can finish the sentence, Mala faints, hitting her head on the table. Bill's voice from the bar, as before.)

BILL: Hey.

ADELE *(To us)*: People rush over, she bounces back up like a cartoon and announces:

MALA: It's nothing.

ADELE *(To us)*: We actually go on bobbing our heads, people are staring, she's sweating— *(To Mala)* When did you move here?

MALA: Last week.

ADELE: Do you have a doctor?

MALA *(Head shake)*: Can we start over? . . . You look really beautiful.

ADELE: You look sweaty and flushed and not at all—

MALA: Unravishing?

ADELE: Should you be traveling?

MALA: Okay, look . . . Maybe— How do I say this without you . . . ?

ADELE: I'll sit, I'll listen.

MALA: Are you sure you're not fooling yourself when you say this critic has nothing to teach you?

ADELE: Teach me?!?!

MALA: Shhhh.

ADELE: That's not how it works!

MALA: Are you sure?

ADELE: YES!

MALA: Well, tell me how it works then, please.

ADELE: It's my life. My life.

MALA: Maybe it shouldn't be?

(Adele is about to bolt.)

Here's what I've learned. If I want to succeed and get out of whatever miserable situation I find myself in, I have to pay attention to how things work and play along.

ADELE: That is not how art is done—

MALA: If someone chosen, hired to speak for the public—

ADELE: The public? The public doesn't speak, the public follows.

MALA: Exactly. And in this instance something a member of the public feels is—

ADELE: You just said you don't know anything about art!

MALA: But he does and if someone wrote that about me, I think I'd—

ADELE: IT DOESN'T MEAN THAT, MALA!

MALA: Stop shouting, please.

ADELE: THEY HATED DE KOONING, THEY HATED VAN GOGH, THEY HATED JENNY HOLZER, THEY HAVE TO BE SHOWN, SOMEONE HAS TO STAND UP AND BE BRAVE AND SAY, "THIS IS ABOUT THE TRUTH," IT IS ALWAYS A STRUGGLE, ALWAYS, EXCEPT FOR THE HACKS WHO PAINT LIKE THE MAGAZINE COVERS, IT'S NEVER EASY, TRUTH IS HARD.

MALA: And so loud.

ADELE: Sometimes they don't even see it until the artist is dead. And gone.

MALA: Well . . . Give me some of that.

ADELE: What?

MALA: Whatever that is.

ADELE: What?

MALA: No. You are right. Why pay for a subscription to something that spits at you, openly or otherwise? Who needs that?

(Mala tears up the newspaper.)

ADELE: Okay, but . . . it's not so easy if I want to sell a painting . . .

MALA: That's what I'm trying to say: Reinvent yourself.

ADELE: As?

MALA: Do you want to spend the rest of your life in that squalid little apartment, how do you make the rent?

ADELE: I sell paintings . . . What?

(A head shake.)

Do you want to order?

MALA: Judy mentioned you loaned her the painting in her home—

ADELE: No—

MALA: —so her husband's clients would see it.

ADELE: He paid me, *well*, maybe she doesn't know.

MALA: I worry about you, I'm not judging you.

ADELE: Do you need more water? Waiter . . . ?

(Mala faints.)

(To us) And that's Mala.

BILL: Want to come upstairs?

ADELE: Sure.

BILL: Come on.

SCENE 5

Bill's loft. Same night as Scene 2, 2007.

ADELE: You live at the top of the universe . . . *(Hits her head on the door frame)* Ow.

BILL: Watch.

(Bill and Adele are blind drunk, falling down and unable to coordinate limbs.)

This was Wang / at Columbia?

ADELE: Wong, yeah.

BILL: The touchy-feely Buddhist / guy.

ADELE: Yeah. Heeee didn't do much for Mala but I loved him.

BILL: Why did you say you didn't remember his name?

ADELE: Wow. You do have walls.

BILL: Be windy in here without.

ADELE: You sure you could live with one of my paintings?

BILL: I'd like to live with all of 'em.

ADELE: That's very gallant, but—

BILL: What would you like to drink?

ADELE: Do you have brandy?

BILL: We'll see!

ADELE: Anything.

(Bill falls.)

Whoops. Some people find them challenging.

BILL: Floors?

ADELE: My paintings.

BILL: Isn't that what we want from art?

ADELE: Apparently not for a lot of folks.

BILL: Fuck 'em, Adele.

ADELE: Oh, I have.

BILL: How 'bout Slivovitz?

ADELE: What's that?

BILL: It's uhhh Yugoslav kind of plum brandy.

(He serves the brandy in fancy crystal glasses.)

ADELE: Sure. You have a lot of books on Jesus for someone who doesn't believe in God.

BILL: Ironic, ain't it?

ADELE: Why?

BILL: Well, let's say he wasn't the Son of God, let's say he didn't rise from the dead, let's say he only went around preaching and got himself killed, he's still the most famous person who ever lived by a long long long shot.

ADELE: Well, who are his contenders? Elvis and Hitler.

BILL: That . . . I hadn't thought of. But he must have had something. A tiny band of followers who were really into whatever he was doing.

ADELE: Like me!

(Bill turns back toward her as she leans in to kiss him, and he hits his eyebrow very hard against Adele's teeth.)

BILL: Whoa.

ADELE: Sorry. Are you okay?

BILL: Yes.

ADELE: Wait, you're bleeding.

BILL: I don't care. Your lip.

ADELE: No, you're really bleeding.

BILL: Your lip, awwww.

ADELE: Ice ice.

BILL: Baby. Oh, who cares?

ADELE: Well, I'd like to kiss you without all that—

BILL: Oh, I've performed cunnilingus on countless women who are, / you know . . .

ADELE: Yeah, okay, well, still—

BILL: Ice—hold on . . .

ADELE: . . . There's . . .

BILL: Yeah, I spilled a little—

ADELE: Just . . .

BILL: Take a seat.

ADELE: I'll help—

BILL: No, don't worry about it—

ADELE: Where do you keep—?

(She falls, grabbing Bill. Now they are both down.)

Ow. Ow.

BILL: Welcome to my humble abode.

ADELE: Let me—

BILL: You are so beautiful.

ADELE: Shut up. You're really cut.

BILL: I'm fine, I don't feel a thing.

ADELE: Do you have . . . ?

BILL: Want some ecstasy?

ADELE: Sure. Oh, it kind of scrambles my brains.

(Adele grabs the bottle of brandy and lifts it over Bill's head.)

BILL: What are you doing?

ADELE: I'm sterilizing it.

(She pours brandy into the cut.)

BILL: FUCK!

ADELE: Sorry, I should have said it would sting.

BILL: OW! OW! OW!

ADELE: Okay, it'll be fine.

BILL: My eye!

ADELE: Oh no.

BILL: Oh, damn. I really am bleeding . . .

ADELE: Me, too.

BILL: Are you okay?

ADELE *(Wave of nausea)*: I'm just a little . . .

BILL: Breathe. You want a pan?

ADELE: Where's the bathroom?

BILL: Through there to the left.

ADELE: More walls, my God . . .

BILL: Here.

ADELE: Oh . . . no . . . I . . . no, I think I'm better.

BILL: Come here.

ADELE: You're all bloody.

BILL: Kiss me.

ADELE: Wait.

(They undress partway.)

Whose blood is this?

BILL *(Finding pills in his pocket)*: Here.

ADELE: Are you trying to get me high?

BILL: Come here.

(He pulls her face over top of him as he lies back.)

ADELE: Wait.

(Bill grabs her face, preventing her from avoiding his lips, which are open, ready to kiss.)

BILL: No more waiting—

ADELE: No, no, I—

(She vomits into his open mouth.)

Oh.

BILL: I wasn't expecting that.

ADELE: Oh, God.

BILL: Wow.

ADELE: Sorry. Listen—

BILL: Okay, let's—regroup.

ADELE: I'll—

BILL: Stay there!

ADELE: I think—

BILL *(Cleaning up)*: Just stay where you are!

ADELE: Do you want help?

BILL: No more helping! . . . *(Answering an earlier question)* Being ahead of the curve is the way to go.

ADELE: What curve?

BILL: You and Jesus.

ADELE: They crucified him.

BILL: He scared them.

ADELE: How?

BILL: Love every other human being as you would yourself?

ADELE: That's scary.

BILL: Like your paintings.

ADELE: Mala hated them. She said they look like torture victims.

BILL: You're not over Mala.

ADELE: Oh believe me, I am over Mala.

BILL: You place beautiful things next to ugly things. It scared her.

(He hands Adele a pill.)

ADELE *(Taking it)*: Embrace what is! That's what Wong said. His definition of joy.

(He is cleaning her up.)

I have to paint tomorrow.

BILL: Good, I got a few bypasses myself.

ADELE: If I miss more than a day, I stop for months, so I can't. I stopped for Mala's illness, and—

MALA'S VOICE: You're going to have to sacrifice something. Either it's me or it's—

(Adele drops the elegant, paper-thin crystal glass, shattering it. She bends over to pick up the broken pieces.)

BILL: Don't touch it.

ADELE: I did it.

BILL: I don't want you to— / Move!

ADELE: Let me, please—

(In the tussle to determine who will take charge, one pushes the other off-balance. Then there is a teetering and they both fall into the shards of broken glass, trying to spare the palms

of hands, elbows, forearms, or knees taking the slices. They are both suddenly bleeding.)

I'm really—shit.

BILL: Oh God, okay, 911 . . .

ADELE: Big deep . . .

BILL: Don't look at the bone . . .

ADELE: This is . . . Bill . . .

BILL: I know.

ADELE: Can we take care of a dog? *(Spinning)* Whoa.

BILL: I save people's lives.

ADELE: Me, too.

BILL: Through art.

ADELE: That is right.

BILL: Motherfuckers.

ADELE: *Fuck.*

BILL: Don't look at it.

(She looks at it. She looks up at Bill. They kiss and begin to make love.
   Interval.)

SCENE 6

Adele alone, painting.

ADELE *(To us)*: I was told not to stare at the wreckage of my past. But when what you do for a living is see, when who you are and why and how and all you are . . .

(Hospital room. Same night as Scene 4, 1999. A documentary plays on the unseen hospital TV. Mala is in bed, in a hospital gown.)

What did that mean, coded?

MALA: Did I say that?

ADELE: You said you coded.

MALA: It meant I died.

ADELE: No really.

MALA: It meant I died.

ADELE: You didn't— / *What?*

MALA: My body shut down. I saw the white light.

ADELE: You didn't see the white light.

MALA: My system collapsed. This isn't your worry.

ADELE: I'm not leaving you here, Mala.

MALA: Go home.

ADELE: No.

MALA: They won't let you stay.

ADELE: They have, and you don't know me.

MALA: You should be painting.

ADELE: You don't care, you hate them.

MALA: Not as much as I hate the idea of you hating me for the ones you're not painting.

ADELE *(Placing a wet cloth on Mala)*: That feel good?

MALA: So good you'd die.

(Adele tries to turn off the TV with the remote.)

Leave it.

ADELE: Oh, you're supposed to fill out nearest of kin—

MALA: I want to hear.

ADELE: Do this first, / they came while you were asleep, I promised.

MALA: No . . . Give it to me. Adele?

ADELE: It's about *torture*.

MALA: I don't care.

(Adele turns up the sound on the TV, sits, sips from a water bottle, and grows more and more hysterical about the TV documentary.)

TV VOICE: . . . their limbs crushed with blunt instruments then threaded through the spokes of the wheel, which was hoisted into the air and left for birds to pick at. An observer described one victim as a "sort of screaming and eyeless puppet, with four loose tentacles like a sea monster of raw, slimy, and shapeless flesh." The breaking wheel was one of the most popular spectacles employed in the public squares of Europe from 1450 to 1750. The masses, both common and noble, watched in fascination, cheering a good wheeling. A woman or a number of women in a row brought even greater enthusiasm.

(Mala shuts off the TV.)

ADELE *(Singing)*: "That's entertainment!" *(Handing Mala the forms)* Next of kin, please.

MALA: I don't speak to my family.

ADELE: Really? Well, I tried to give them my name, they said you had to—put me down.

MALA: None of this is your affair, Adele, go home, your breath stinks of alcohol.

ADELE: So?

MALA: The world doesn't think your art is valuable so I'll be your purpose?

ADELE: No, Mala—

MALA: Go paint and leave me be, I'm fine—

ADELE: I am not / going to abandon you—

MALA: You've got it in your water bottle. What kind of a care-taker would you actually be?

ADELE: You can't scare me away.

MALA: Interesting point: What's the difference between a serial killer and an active alcoholic?—

ADELE: I'm not an—

MALA: In fact? Nothing. They're both killing people.

ADELE: I think that's— / just a bit . . .
MALA: Of course you do.

(*Beat.*)

ADELE: No. Here, good, you're absolutely right, I'll stop—

(*She pours the water bottle out into the sink.*)

MALA: Not for me you won't.
ADELE: I'm stopping. For me. You're worth it to me.
MALA: You don't know me.
ADELE: And you don't know me. I've been looking for a reason, you're giving me one . . . Good. I'm not taking another drink.
MALA: Until?
ADELE: Until—I don't know . . . Until you're out of here, / okay, how's that?
MALA: Ah-ha, well. You can start right up again at the morgue. / Great.
ADELE: What are you—? . . . What does that mean?
MALA: I'm tired.
ADELE: The morgue?

(*Time jump. Dr. Wong, seen only in silhouette, stands in the doorway to the room.*)

DR. WONG: We'll have results in a few days and until then it's important that you know—
MALA: Yes yes yes, thank you, I don't need to be . . .
DR. WONG: Of course, I understand, you've been a nurse—And (*To Adele*) you are partners?

ADELE: Yes.   MALA: No.

DR. WONG: Please call me if you have any concerns at all. I'm here and on call all night. I'll stop back.

ADELE: Thank you. *So much!*

DR. WONG: Good-bye, Mala.

(Mala says nothing as Dr. Wong moves off.)

ADELE: Wasn't he amazing?

MALA: Because he dawdled?

ADELE: Dawdled? Is / that—?

MALA: You have to wonder why he wasn't in more of a hurry.

ADELE: What was that thing he said? Large my . . . eye—

MALA: Giant cell myocarditis.

ADELE: What's that?

MALA: That's what he hopes it isn't.

ADELE: Why?

MALA: I would need a heart transplant. Getting a heart is like, "Come back with the broomstick of the Wicked Witch of the West." They're going to want me out of here.

ADELE: You are too beautiful for anyone to want you gone.

MALA: Would you please give it up?

ADELE: I haven't had a drink since you asked. You think I wasn't serious? What if I love you, Mala?

(A sigh.)

I'm not going to be whatever nightmare you faced in your family. I won't be. You think painting the way I have in the face of decades of criticism—

MALA: Okay.

ADELE: —is an indication of weakness? You think I don't have resolve? I can't hang on like a motherfucking / leech?

MALA: Leech?

ADELE: You'll see. I will not let you down. Whatever your family did or was I will show you what a true family is. What love means. You'll see.

(Time jump. A new morning.)

Hey. Guess what!

MALA: Don't tell me they found a heart lying out in the hall.

ADELE: There may be one in this hospital.

MALA: Impossible.

ADELE: Not so.

MALA: A human heart in this joint?

ADELE: Mm-hm.

MALA: Really?

ADELE: I just spoke to Wong.

MALA: Are you giving head to the medical board?

ADELE: Isn't that incredible?

MALA: I can't be at the top of the list.

ADELE: It's your blood type, it's a fluke.

MALA: I don't want a fluke's heart.

ADELE: See? Not everything is / so—

MALA: What will happen to mine?

ADELE: Heart? I don't know. We'll ask him.

MALA: But . . . what if he gives me the Wong answer?

ADELE: Oh God, honey! He won't, he'll give you all the wight ones. But you have to be strong.

MALA: Breathe on me.

(She holds Adele's face in her hands.)

ADELE: See?

(Time jump. Mala is asleep, post-op. Everything is beeping and humming. Adele, wearing a surgical mask, hugs Dr. Wong, also in a mask.)

DR. WONG: You rest.

ADELE: Thank you thank you thank you thank you.

DR. WONG: Rest.

ADELE: You.

(Adele gives him one more hug. He leaves. Adele checks on Mala, then reaches into her own bag, takes out a pill, and swallows it without water.)

MALA: Show me.

ADELE: Hey!

MALA: Show me a painting.

ADELE: Oh. My photos?

MALA: Yeah.

ADELE: How do you feel?

MALA: I'll tell you . . . Let me see . . .

ADELE: He said you wouldn't wake for hours probably . . .

MALA: Well, now we know how much he knows.

ADELE: Stop.

(Adele finds photos of her paintings for Mala to see.)

MALA: Didn't work.

ADELE: What?

MALA: My new heart.

ADELE: It's working.

MALA: I still hate them.

(Pause.)

Didn't work.

SCENE 7

Bill's loft. Another night, 2008.

BILL: Hey! Hey hey! He really liked them!
ADELE: You don't know that.
BILL: I do.
ADELE: How?
BILL: He just texted.
ADELE: He did?

(Bill shows her the text.)

"I really like them!" My God. Do we have any more?
BILL: He'll tell MoMA and Larry and Doug and the Whitney
    and / Moe and Curly and—
ADELE: You don't know.
BILL: —and people will start buying.
ADELE: You don't know that.
BILL: Yes.
ADELE: Do we have any more?
BILL: Yes, I do, and yes, I do— *(Giving Adele an estasy)* I heard
    you, you're doing that thing where you—
ADELE: No, I heard you.
BILL: —check out for a / couple of seconds.
ADELE: I heard you, but I just—I wish you hadn't told Klaus all
    that religious shit.

(Bill gives her another ecstasy.)

Thank you.
BILL: They / need a hook.
ADELE: I heard you—but it will be in every review and—

BILL: Yeah? So?

ADELE: I mean, if he doesn't just forget about me by the time he gets home.

BILL: Why do you have to blow apart everything good? Be happy! He *REALLY* liked them. I've never heard him use that word. People need someone to contextualize things for them!

ADELE: It doesn't work like that.

BILL: Oh, no? *(Beat)*

ADELE *(To us)*: What I didn't know about the world . . . or me.

(Time jump. Adele has the hiccups. Bill has a copy of the New York Times Sunday Magazine *with the headline on the cover:)*

BILL: "The New Spiritual Vision."

ADELE *(Covering her ears)*: Lalalalalalala!

(She pours a tall drink.)

BILL: Hey hey hey hey. *(Sees the dog)* Look who's happy!

ADELE: Me? / Not really.

BILL: Look who else! / Hey, you! Yes! YEEEEESSSSS! Lick lick lick!

ADELE *(Overlapping, to the dog)*: Hello, you! . . . He adores you.

BILL: Wait.

ADELE: What?

BILL: Come here, you have a . . . *(Makes as if he is going to remove something from her cheek or clothing, then startles her)* Boo!

(Pause. Hiccup. She starts to drink her enormous drink from the opposite lip.)

Hey hey hey hey, you want another blackout?

ADELE: Yes, if I'm good and truly deserve it.

SCENE 8

Mala's apartment. Night, Y2K.
Mala is lighting candles. Adele is sketching.

MALA: We need to move the heaters next to the pipes and the faucets should be left dripping at all times so the pipes don't accidentally freeze.

ADELE: Do pipes ever freeze on purpose?

MALA: What? Even if the rest of the building has their faucets off, if we keep ours dripping then we stand a better chance of having water.

ADELE: Even without power? To . . . push it up the . . . ?

MALA: I don't know about that.

ADELE: I've got your love to keep me warm.

MALA: Yeah, try that at Auschwitz.

ADELE: Will there be like a wormhole and we'll go back in time?

MALA: Are you high on something?

ADELE: I'm trying my bestest, honey, to encourage a calm, sane approach toward the future.

MALA: The future may just be *Lord of the Flies*.

ADELE: The idea that all the brilliant people who brought us computers and email were collectively incapable of imagining a number higher than ninety-nine or a century other than their own, it's just— Sit, have a drink. He said you can have wine.

MALA: It's not a good time to test it.

ADELE *(Singing)*: "Off with my overcoat, off with my glove. I need no overcoat! I'm burning with love! My heart's / on fire!"[1]

---

1. Any song can work here as long as it's about staying warm; this lyric is only provided as an example.

MALA: Okay, stop it, you're driving me crazy. What are those pills in your bag?

ADELE: What pills?

(Mala picks up Adele's bag, begins looking.)

Were you looking for something?

MALA: Yes.

ADELE: I am starting to hear a message.

MALA: These.

ADELE: I don't even remember, what does it say?

MALA: Lipitor, but these aren't Lipitor.

ADELE: I stopped taking the statins, remember?

MALA: Yes, so what are these?

ADELE: I don't know, what's the date on the . . . ?

MALA: There were more last week.

ADELE: Noooo. The message I hear is I couldn't possibly be my real, true, honest, unmedicated self if I'm happy and calm. That could be understood to be an offensive message, if one were inclined to hear it that way. Which I am not. Do you want me to be taking pills?

MALA: What's the champagne for?

ADELE: Us. You.

MALA: What was in the freezer?

ADELE: It's supposed to be a surprise.

MALA: Hit me.

ADELE: Let's wait to see if the National Guard starts clubbing illegal aliens before we move to the celebration, okay? . . . I'd like to point out—

MALA: Just tell me what those rotted vines are, okay, I can tell they're . . .

(Silence.)

ADELE: —that it's past midnight.

MALA: . . . Well, looks like we're going to have to have a sale on lanterns and tamales.

ADELE: Well, canned tamales, as far as I'm concerned, are an eternal joy and will never wear out their promise of delight. There will be other potential catastrophic scenarios ahead, I promise, darling. Don't be blue.

MALA: What's the surprise?

ADELE: Wait, are you actually mad that the world didn't come to an end? . . .

MALA: No! Stop it, shut up! I want to break up.

(Outside, horns are honking and people are shouting "Happy New Year!")

ADELE: Happy New Year!

MALA: Happy New Year! . . . I do, I want to break up.

ADELE: And you were waiting . . . ?

MALA: I didn't want you to be alone if there was rioting or violence. I don't think you can take care of yourself.

(Pause.)

ADELE: Say more.

MALA: I'm not seeing anyone else, I'll find another place, I'll help with the rent, I'd rather it not be a big giant drama, I just . . . want to break up.

(Pause. Adele gets up and stirs the pot on the stove.)

ADELE: Do you want some tamales?

MALA: No, thank you.

(Adele opens the champagne, pours a glass, and sips it.)

You *were* quitting for me.

ADELE: You are not leaving me in a moment of apocalyptic disappointment, Mala.

MALA: I'm sorry I didn't wait till tomorrow, if that would have been better.

ADELE: It is tomorrow. I'm boiling up a pot of ayahuasca, which I have been saving from before I met you, and I am going to take in the magnitude of the new era, that came without technological horror, no blood running in the streets, and though you so obviously would like some blood running through here, it is not going to be mine.

MALA: You think I'm such a bitch.

ADELE: You think you are such a bitch. Bitch is a word like "shy" or "crazy" that people use to excuse never unpacking what they are really doing or taking responsibility—

MALA: Stop lecturing me all the time, stop it!

ADELE: Go. Somewhere else. And make.

MALA: You are taking some kind / of—

ADELE: —someone else.

MALA: . . . drug or . . .

ADELE: —feel bad.

MALA: Your pupils are dilated.

(Mala begins to pack up things into an overnight bag. Adele takes out a bag of leaves and puts them into boiling water.)

A pot of what?

ADELE: It's an Amazonian plant preparation used in Divine rites.

MALA: Uh-huh. My dad? Was by all accounts a nice enough guy when he wasn't drinking but since that was never I didn't meet the nice guy.

ADELE: I've been completely sober for months. It's the turn of the millennium.

MALA: You can't have thought it would be okay for me to take, is it a hallucinogen?

ADELE: It's considered a medicine. It's been used for centuries, you open your eyes whenever you don't want to see the visions, they stop. Maybe this isn't the best night to seek the Divine, never mind. And thank you for telling me about your dad.

MALA: Oh, you ain't heard nothing.

ADELE: I assumed something very bad happened, and I'm sorry.

MALA: I was such an idiot for opening up to you, I knew it wasn't safe, I knew it.

ADELE: I'm never going to let you down.

MALA: You have let me down.

ADELE: Tell me how.

MALA: By lying to me.

ADELE: That's a very serious charge to level at someone who has been here night and day—

MALA: And I told you you would use that against me.

ADELE: I'm not using it—

MALA: You know nothing about the meaning of words, what they truly represent, you live in your mind.

ADELE: You want me to throw it away?

MALA: I'm not gonna tell you—

ADELE: Tell me what you want.

MALA: I want to break up.

(*Beat. Adele drinks the ayahuasca brew.*)

ADELE (*To us*): I could fight for my paintings. I could fight for Mala's survival. But when it came to my own . . .

(*Time jump. Adele is vomiting into the sink, with Mala holding her hair back.*)

It's okay, it's part of the ritual.

MALA: I can see the attraction.

ADELE: I'm gonna be fine, you can go.

MALA: I don't want to go, you know that. But you have to make a choice: me, or booze and drugs.

ADELE: Why do I have to choose?

MALA: Because. I love you too much to watch you do this, and I want to live in a safe home.

ADELE: I think we have a safe home.

MALA: I have sacrificed so much to be here in this moment with this life . . . And you are going to have to sacrifice something, either it's me or those things. Choose.

ADELE: No.

(Pause.)

MALA: Sure.

(Mala turns away, starts to do something, then wheels on Adele.)

What the fuck is wrong with you?!?!

ADELE: Why are you shouting?

MALA: YOU SHOUT! WHENEVER YOU WANT AND ABOUT STUPID SHIT LIKE ART! ART SHOULD NOT BE SHOUTED ABOUT! SURVIVAL, LOVE, EXISTENCE, HEALTH SHOULD BE SHOUTED ABOUT! LOVE AND TRUST! You're a drunk like any other drunk!

(Mala grabs Adele.)

ADELE: I'm calling the police.

MALA: Call! I want 'em here! I'm not eating vines, you are.

ADELE: This relentless twelve-step bullshit—

MALA: I don't have all those pills in my bag, you do, you think I am stupid enough not to notice! You're flushed. Your promises are shit, you imagine you don't and haven't and won't continue to trip and fall down stairs and face-plant—

ADELE: I'm clumsy.

MALA: Just because you hate yourself you have to make everyone else do it, too.

ADELE: I'd like you to leave before I start having—

MALA: Right. Good. Remember those words.

ADELE: You already broke up with me.

MALA: No. You never were here. Ever.

(Mala leaves the room. Adele is alone.)

SCENE 9

Park. Day, 2009.
   Bill is there. Adele, nicely pulled together, approaches.

ADELE: Thank you for doing this. Hey. *(Goes to kiss him)* May I—?

(Bill pulls away.)

Okay.

(Silence. She has a piece of paper, which she unfolds, smooths out, stares at. Bill offers a sip from his thermos.)

How are you?

BILL: Am I your first?

ADELE: No, I did the others.

BILL: Mala?

ADELE: My sponsor said I should leave her be.

BILL: But not me?

ADELE: No, I guess . . . Dad was the hardest. By far. Yeah. He died.

BILL: I was / at the funeral—

ADELE: Oh, that's right. Sorry. I'm— He was in that place, assisted living. I don't think you saw. It . . . Well, it got bad. Whenever he couldn't find his TV remote, he'd call 911. But . . . I tried to, I wrote it out, like this, thought he would just read it? *(Dad's voice) "You read it."* With his deafness, I thought, "Let's go for a drive." *"No."* "Please?" *"Say what you have to say!"* I start reading, you know, "I stole from you and Mom." *"What?!?!"* *(Louder)* "I stole from you and Mommy!" . . . I was afraid he'd die and I'd drink over it. Which is why you do it, it's for—

BILL: Is there anything about me you do remember?

ADELE: Oh, that's right. I'm just . . . very nervous, Bill. I know it's hard for you, too—

BILL: You don't.

ADELE: Don't what?

BILL: Don't presume.

ADELE: Oh. Okay.

(Pause. She fingers the handwritten list, staring down.)

This is, you don't have to say anything. You know. I was drunk the first time we went home; I threw up on you.

BILL: On?

ADELE: In. Your open mouth, you wouldn't let me turn my head. You were trying to kiss me, I know. Yes. I was wrong. These are all, I was wrong, each of these, and I'm sorry. I exploited you, letting you be my patron . . . And you know I'm grateful for everything good that's happened; I would never have / found—

BILL: Stick to the list.

ADELE: I will, okay, I wouldn't have a gallery without you. Or this security. I used you. I drank through your whole treatment; I was not there for you, and even though everything has turned out— You're still in . . . ? You're still in remission, aren't you? . . . Bill?

BILL: This isn't about me.

ADELE: But . . . Can't I know? . . . Okay. You look well. *(No response)* Fine. I was not fully there. I was angry at you for being sick, what were you doing getting sick? You're a doctor . . . I called you Peter while we were making love. I don't even remember who Peter was. I remembered his peter, I messed around with—Madeline?

BILL: My office manager?

ADELE: At that Christmas party. She was very sweet about it. I'd given her ten ecstasies practically, it was nothing.

BILL: No reviews, please.

ADELE: Yes.

(Silence. Her cell phone buzzes; she glances at it.)

BILL: New victim?

ADELE: Mala, texting to say that she won't meet.

BILL: I thought your sponsor said to leave her alone.

ADELE: It's . . . It's a suggestion.

(Beat.)

Okay. I banged up the car. Totaled. More than once. I . . . didn't read all the Kierkegaard—at the time, I have since. I lied. I can't remember all the lies.

BILL: How 'bout you give me the big ones.

ADELE: You want the Greatest Hits? Okay . . . Or you can just— . . . It really is good to see you . . . I stole Fentanyl from your office, I stole morphine. I took Marcus's anti-convulsants, the phenobarb, one pill in three seemed to keep him . . .

(Pause.)

BILL: Say it.

(Pause.)

ADELE: I can't . . .
BILL: You—
ADELE: I . . .

(Silence.)

. . . ran over Marcus. I knew you didn't believe me. You were well and . . . I . . . think I believed it, some neighbor. I needed to believe it, so I had a separate . . . The collar had fallen off, he ran through the electric fence . . . That was what happened. I . . . felt the bump; I drove to the animal hospital, he was in my lap, I kept thinking, it's going to be okay, I hated myself so much. He was all that was good in us, I loved him. I did. I think that's it. I peed in the bed one night when I couldn't bother to get up and—
BILL: So you put his body on the / street like trash.
ADELE: Yes. Yes, I did that.
BILL: And made all those fliers—
ADELE: Yes.
BILL: —about obeying the speed limit. And—
ADELE: Yes, yes—
BILL: —dumped me, too. Like trash.
ADELE: Yes.

BILL: I was relieved when you slept with other people because then I didn't have to feel bad that nobody would buy your work.

ADELE: . . . I didn't know that.

BILL: They're you. Your paintings.

ADELE: Yes.

BILL: Who would want to live with that? So much beauty and then that stinking, rotting bullshit right down front and center.

ADELE: Right.

BILL: You are an unmitigated, yes, gold-digging, sad, pathetic, underdeveloped, bloodsucking cunt who plays the victim at every turn and uses anybody she can and never keeps her word—

ADELE: Yes.

BILL: —and never makes the world any better and holds herself to no standards and—

ADELE: I didn't.

BILL: —takes and takes and takes and—

ADELE: I was like that.

BILL: Was? You're no different. You don't take on board the reality of another person. Teaching *me* about the reasons behind making amends. Telling me your dad died?

ADELE: I'm nervous.

BILL: Making excuses to release you from admitting to being who you are.

(Silence.)

ADELE: Okay. Well—

BILL: Your jokes are lame and your body is repulsive and you make me ashamed of myself for having even bothered to flirt with you the first time I set eyes on you and thinking, "Wouldn't it be fun to burst into tears and make this woman love me?"

ADELE: You did not do that. You did not do that . . . You're saying anything . . .

BILL: Get away from me.

ADELE: Wait. I have one . . . I have a problem, Bill. I'm still very much in love with you. And I miss you. And I want to try again. Because I don't believe any of that.

BILL: You said I was insane for asking if you ran over him. Mentally ill.

ADELE: I did.

BILL: For even wondering such a cruel, sadistic, paranoid—

ADELE: Yes, yes, it was wrong, I admit, it was wrong, I was wrong.

BILL: Pretty, pretty part. Paint the pretty part brighter, the shit is still stinking. It keeps on putrefying. You called me a worm. And a drunk. And an ecstasy addict.

ADELE: You are an addict, Bill. And I was, too. Addicts lie.

BILL: No, you, don't tell me what I do. Even if it's just "A Suggestion."

ADELE: It's, okay, me, I lie, I lied, it's a disease, it's—

BILL: It's not a disease, it's a choice.

ADELE: Okay.

BILL: People with cancer can't *stop* having cancer. You stopped. You chose it. That's not a disease. Who would choose to have a disease? It's bad science. To call it a disease. I would never quit, or choose to quit drinking for you.

ADELE: Of course not. That's isn't mine to—

BILL: I would make no sacrifices for you.

ADELE: Okay. But I will . . . I will work if you . . . I'm putting it out there. That's all. That's all. I'm putting it out. I love you.

BILL: Define love. What is love to you? That your higher power now?

ADELE: Love is what makes me believe I can start again, that we could start again, and that I could deserve you and you and I could deserve . . . It's the impossible thing Kierkegaard talks about.

BILL: Kierkegaard's impossible thing has only to do with a man who was crucified and rose again, a nonperson by any standard so inconsequential from a town with no roads who couldn't read whose family knew he was crazy, an outcast even among the most outcast, *Jews*, a nobody's nobody who said, "Give away all your money and only do for others," and even though he had no money or property or influence, they still had to kill him. That's what Kierkegaard's impossible thing is.

ADELE: Okay. Okay, Bill. I love you. I will always / love—

(He hits her with real force, sudden and very sharp. Silence.)

I love you. You can't hit me. But I love you. And that's the deal.

(Silence.)

Your turn . . . Bill? . . .

(Silence.)

Forgive me.

BILL: Define forgiveness.

ADELE: Forgiving is giving up the option for revenge. I forgive you.

BILL: For?

ADELE: Feeding me drugs from the night we met and going to work hungover every day and caring for people including me in . . . an altered state and using your money and power to keep everything safe and numb and within your control.

BILL: Why would you love someone like that?

ADELE: 'Cause that's the kind of gal *I'm.*

SCENE 10

Adele's building. Late afternoon, 2014.
  Adele is alone, again returning to the large, unseen canvas.

ADELE *(To us)*: We are what we practice, did you know that? Not what we say, or feel, recommend . . . I have my daily ritual, sometimes hourly, bi-minutely: I ask to be able to—and willing—to travel the greatest distance of all: from here *(Touches her head)* to here. *(Touches her heart)* Very hard.

(She closes her eyes and silently asks for the willingness to travel that very distance. Buzzer.)

My assistant. So. You ready? On your mark, get set.

(She moves to answer the buzzer, the movement causing her such excruciating agony, she lets loose with:)

AAAAAAAAAAAAAAAA! Don't worry, I'm not gonna scream the whole time, it helps me to let it out, you'll come to love it, I do, it's the last scene and it's only shingles. Mine, not the building's. I'm not dying at this moment so we're not winning any Pulitzers either. When I was five I thought it was—I swear: the Pulitt *Surprise!*

(The door opens and Mala peers in.)

MALA: Adele?

(Adele closes her eyes. "It's not possible.")

Adele? . . . It's Mala . . . Can I . . . ? . . . Can you hear me?
ADELE: I'm trying not to turn my neck too fast.
MALA: Oh, can I . . . ?
ADELE: Sure.
MALA: Why . . . ? Are you okay?
ADELE: Yeah.
MALA: It's . . . good to see you. It's been a very long time.
ADELE: Fourteen years.
MALA: Can I . . . ?
ADELE: Careful.

(Mala gingerly opens her arms to embrace Adele, which she does. This, unfortunately, is much more pressure and movement than Adele anticipated, and she releases her most bloodcurdling scream yet:)

AAAAAAAAAA!!!
MALA: Oh, God, honey—
ADELE: It's shingles, it's nothing, help yourself to—
MALA: Shingles?
ADELE: Yeah, pull up a . . . floor.
MALA: I'm fine. What is wrong?
ADELE: Nothing, this is the high point of my life so far, honest
    to *(Volume exploding) Christ FUCK.*
MALA: You look— Well, you look . . . terrible.
ADELE: Do we want to start with how bad I look?
MALA: Why are you holding your head like that?
ADELE: Because it hurts.
MALA: Are you on painkillers?
ADELE: Yes.

MALA: What are you taking?

ADELE: Paint.

MALA: You're sniffing it?

(A look.)

    Well, I don't know.

ADELE: Why are you here?

MALA: . . . I . . .

ADELE: How did you find me?

MALA: Dr. Rubenstein?

ADELE: How do you know Bill?

MALA: He's my doctor.

ADELE: What happened to Wong?

MALA: He died.

ADELE: He did? When?

MALA: Last year.

ADELE: Oh. I loved him.

MALA: He was cracked.

ADELE: He was lovely. Oh, he died? Wait, Bill told you about . . .

MALA: Mm-hm.

ADELE: . . . us?

MALA: Oh. Us?

ADELE: No?

MALA: He . . . told me you were sick.

ADELE: How does he know?

MALA: I don't know, I just started with him . . . He asked if I happened to know you, you'd mentioned me? He suggested I see you right away.

(Adele drops the paintbrush. Mala reaches for it.)

ADELE: Don't. *(Bends down, releasing pain)* AAAAAAAAAAAAA-AAAAGOD-IN-JESUS-FUCK! FUCK-CHRIST-GOD!

MALA: He said you have bone cancer.

ADELE: This is shingles.

MALA: Why would you lie to me?

ADELE: A lot's changed since we saw each other. Lying is not an integral part of my current— I'm actually doing really well, I don't carry around as much anger and blame as I used to.

MALA: Do you or do you not have cancer?

ADELE: I do have cancer, I'm in remission, this is shingles. It's caused from— *(Another surge of pain)* GodDAMMIT! From the— *(Another surge, worse, a tsunami of seething, burning, boiling pain)* CHEMOTHERAPY AND RADIA-TION AND STRESS AND BLAME AND ANGER MAKE IT WORSE, CUNT CUNT CUNT! Not you.

MALA: I think you're lying.

ADELE: Cunt.

MALA: I was a nurse, honey. I have seen shingles.

ADELE: WELL YOU HAVEN'T SEEN *THESE*!!! *FUCK!*

MALA *(Fishing for her cell phone)*: I'm calling Dr. Rubenstein.

ADELE: No! Jesus! He's not my doctor!

MALA: Who's your doctor?

ADELE: Not Bill! Bill and I are divorced.

(Silence.)

Twice.

(Beat.)

I ran over our dog. I puked in his mouth. I ruined alco-hol once and for all for him—drugs, alcohol, marriage, love, children. We have a kid. Justin. From our second marriage. I had ovarian torsion during my first trimes-ter, the pain was unbearable, they put me on painkillers and anti-anxiety meds. It went from bad to nightmare, I drank, I smoked crack. Bill didn't know. He got sober. He got custody. I wasn't allowed to see Justin for the first two years until I could prove I was clean. He's sweet, they don't know yet if he's normal—Justin, not Bill—he's five. He's got full-time care and lives with Bill. I see him every other week. Bill and I don't interact, which I *(Sharp pain)* HATE!

MALA: I want you to take—

ADELE: NO!

MALA: —something.

ADELE: NO!

MALA: Gabapentin isn't addictive, here.

ADELE: No, Mala, thank you.

MALA: I can't bear this.

ADELE: Then leave! You're not an addict and you haven't been on my very special journey, but I'm duty-bound to feel this pain because I am not dying. If I were, I'd take the pills, but I'm not, so I'm sticking with my fate, embracing it. Joy!

(Mala is surreptitiously texting on her cell phone.)

My amends to you are on the laptop, folder marked "Mala."

MALA: I don't need you to make amends.

ADELE: It's for me, you don't have to read them.

MALA: You saved my life, Adele.

ADELE: No, I didn't.

MALA: Yes, I was ready to give up, you wouldn't let me.

(Beat.)

That is what's true. I couldn't face the hospitals, knowing what goes on and knowing I wouldn't ever stand a chance of getting a heart in time.

(Short pause.)

ADELE: Well . . . The amends are for me, not you.

(Mala at last begins to take in the paintings all around.)

MALA: Can you email them?
ADELE: Sure.
MALA: Thanks.

(Mala is overwhelmed by the paintings.)

They're beautiful.
ADELE: What? My *paintings*? Who are you?
MALA: They seem different. Or maybe, I don't know, maybe I understand them now.
ADELE: Why?
MALA: I read a review?
ADELE: This is where I kill you.
MALA: I'm sorry. I needed to understand.
ADELE: Go.
MALA: Please?
ADELE: Please.
MALA: May I stay? I'll be good.

(Beat.)

You know I'm married?
ADELE: No.
MALA: We have two kids.
ADELE: What does . . . ?
MALA: Debbie? Do? Not Dallas. She's a cop. They're all having lunch at the corner . . . I saw you on PBS. You were so eloquent. Well . . . I always knew you would break through.

ADELE: WHAT?!?!

(Buzzer.)

That's my assistant, just push the . . .

(Buzzer overlaps Adele's line. Mala gathers her things.)

MALA: It might be them.
ADELE: No, just—
MALA: I'll go down.
ADELE: You don't need to, / Mala.
MALA: I want to.

(Mala goes out the door and heads down the stairs.)

ADELE *(To us)*: I'd give anything to rise up from my pain and
float after her and rip her scalp off the way the lovely native
people did, ow ow, skip to now, skip skip—AAAAAAAA!
(She tries deep breaths) I am grateful for today, I am grateful
for a chance to be grateful, to paint, to live another day
and feel this pain, to reach out to another human being—

(Knock on the door. From off:)

BILL'S VOICE: Hey.
ADELE *(To us)*: —just not that one.

(Bill enters, followed by Mala.)

BILL: Hey.
ADELE: Hey.
BILL: I—
ADELE: Where's my assistant?

BILL: I don't—I . . .

MALA: I'm going to run down to the deli and pop back in two seconds.

BILL: Okay.

MALA: Is there . . . *(Locates a key hanging by the door)* Is this the key? Adele? I'll just . . . *(Taking the key)* Okay.

(Mala descends the stairs.)

BILL: I won't stay.

(Adele paints.)

May I see?

ADELE: Who told you?

BILL: It's a small world. May I look?

ADELE: Doctors.

BILL: May I?

ADELE: What's stopping you?

BILL: No, at your shingles—

ADELE: You don't believe me either.

BILL: No, I do.

ADELE: Then no, there's no need. And I hope it wasn't my doctor who told you I'm dying because then he's lying to me. I have shingles.

BILL: Okay.

ADELE: Look, love . . . we have managed not to hurt each other more . . .

BILL: We haven't seen each other.

ADELE: Exactly. And I'm trying—so hard . . . It's . . . I'm in such . . .

BILL: It's okay.

ADELE: . . . Just to do the right thing . . . AAAAAAAAAAAAAAA!

BILL: I know.

ADELE: HOW THE FUCK ARE YOU?

BILL: I'm okay.

ADELE: Good. So. Mala.

BILL: Yeah.

ADELE: How's Justin?

BILL: Oh, he fell, he got stitches.

ADELE: Where?

BILL: On his face.

ADELE: Where?

BILL: Here. Here. And here.

ADELE: Ohhh. Baby . . .

BILL: What can I do?

ADELE: . . . why did you . . . ? No, I'm always—I went right to
the thought that you let him fall—

BILL: Yeah. No. So you won't take pain medications.

ADELE: NO!

BILL: You taking Acyclovir?

ADELE: Yes.

BILL: You taking—

ADELE: Yes, I'm taking everything I can.

BILL: We don't want to see you in pain.

ADELE: Well, someone does.

*(She paints. Bill stands in awe before the painting Adele is
working on.)*

BILL: Is this a triptych?

ADELE: Mm-hm.

BILL: Does it have a title?

ADELE: Yeah.

(Silence.)

BILL: What?

ADELE: Golgotha!

BILL: . . . I thought you didn't like the religious angle. So describe the pain.

ADELE: You're not my doctor, Bill!

(He starts toward the door.)

What does Christ say?

BILL: About?

ADELE: I don't know, figs? Anything.

BILL: Well, actually, they've done textual analyses of all the Gospels and—

ADELE: Uh-huh?

BILL: —the Gnostic texts—

ADELE: Right.

BILL: —and the Dead Sea Scrolls and think they can more or less isolate those things he may actually have said.

ADELE: This from the faithless one . . . Don't tell me you've found a higher power.

BILL: Well, you know what they say in AA.

ADELE: What?

BILL: "How the fuck did I end up in this church basement?"

(Adele laughs, which causes more pain.)

ADELE: JESUS!

BILL: He might have said, "Not to worry, tomorrow will take care of itself." He said, "The Kingdom of God is in us."

ADELE: Oh, boy.

BILL: "Only people who don't know God worry." "Let the dead bury their dead."

ADELE *("What does that even mean?")*: Good?

BILL: He said, "Don't condemn others."

ADELE: No.

BILL: He said, "Be afraid of / no one."

ADELE *(More pain)*: Aaaaaa—sorry.

BILL: That's / okay.

ADELE *(Prompting him)*: "Be afraid of no one."

BILL: "People can kill you but they cannot harm your soul." He said, "I come to bring trouble, not peace."

ADELE: Haha, aaaaaaAAAAAAAAAAAAAA! Oh, it's bad now, this is the worst.

BILL: He said, "If we try to save our life we will lose it."

ADELE: Skip to now. Skip to now! GO AHEAD, *PLEASE*!

BILL: "Don't worry about the food you put in your mouth, worry about the words that come out of it." He said, "Do not murder."

ADELE: God! Kill me anyway.

(Mala has returned with a bottle of pear juice. She observes.)

BILL: "Be faithful in marriage."

ADELE: Fuck you.

BILL: "Do not tell lies about others." "Respect your father and mother."

ADELE: Shit.

BILL: "Love others as much as you love yourself."

ADELE: Oy.

BILL: "And if you want to be perfect," he said, "go sell everything you own." "Give the money to the poor, and don't take any oaths, let your 'yes' mean yes and your 'no' mean no." He said, "Don't brag about your good deeds." He said, "Pray in private." He said, "You see these buildings? They will most certainly be torn down." He said, "Follow me." He said, "I am so sad, I feel as if I am dying." He said, "My God, my God, why have you forsaken me?" He said, "Will you marry me?"

ADELE: Christ said?

BILL: Nah, that was Rubenstein.

ADELE *(Laughs)*: Three time's a charm? . . .

(She resumes painting.)

BILL: Will you?

ADELE: Yeah.

MALA: You people are so fucked, okay? Just sayin'.

(Adele keeps painting from now on.)

ADELE: I can live with it, I can live the pain. True joy is acceptance.

MALA: That's what Wong said!

ADELE *(To us)*: May you find joy. That's all I've got. Firmly secure your own mask before helping others. Love yourself first. Try to forgive. *(She turns to Mala)* What else?

MALA *(Holds up pear juice)*: Eat well.

(Adele looks to Bill.)

BILL: He said, "Is this hummus bad?"

ADELE *(To us)*: Joy.

(Bill and Mala watch as Adele paints. As the light fades, she is hit with more bursts of pain:)

Joy, motherfuckers! JOY!

(Adele, Bill and Mala look at Adele's painting.)

END OF PLAY